A Grandpa Bale Guide

A POCKET FULL OF PUFFINS

Jim Bale and Gregg Solms

ISBN: 9798465782913
Imprint: Independently Published

All photographs were taken by the authors.

For children and grandchildren everywhere!

We thank our children and grandchildren for their love and inspiration, and our wives, Martha and Wendy, for their support and thoughtful suggestions.

Grandpa Bale Guides

A Pocket Full of Puffins
    with Gregg Solms

Animals of the World: What's my name?
Stories in Stone: An introduction to rock art.

A POCKET FULL OF PUFFINS

Jim Bale and Gregg Solms

One lonely puffin sitting on a rock,
looking for his friends and the rest of the flock.

Two happy puffins, standing side-by-side.
We wonder what they caught on the incoming tide.

Three friendly puffins, one-two-three.
They're living on an island surrounded by the sea.

Four more puffins, what do you know!
They're standing all together in a nice straight row.

Five hungry puffins, looking for some eels.
How they'd like to eat them for their evening meals.

Six resting puffins, lying in the sun.
Soon they'll all be leaving, one by one.

Seven sitting puffins, can you see them all?
One should be careful, so he doesn't slip and fall.

Eight smiling puffins, looking right at you.
What would they do if you told them all to shoo?

Nine swimming puffins, bobbing on a wave.
The ocean's mighty cold; they must be very brave.

Now we have more puffins. Be careful where you walk.
Wake a sleeping puffin, and you'll really hear him squawk.

More about Puffins
from Pétur Puffin
(with help from his friends, Grandpa Bale and Granddaddy Solms)

Pétur Puffin (Consultant)

Where do puffins live?

The North Atlantic Ocean is where we are found.
In "Down East" Maine and Canada - all 'round.
Through Iceland and Russia and Europe, you see,
Puffins range far and wide; such travelers are we!
In summer we nest in caves or the ground.
Good places to live; all quite safe and sound!
In fall through winter, we swim the North Sea,
Though cold and windy, there's lots to eat and plenty to see!

What do puffins like to eat?

We puffins need lots of small fish to eat.
Sand eels, herring, and cod - they're our treat!
Mollusks, marine worms and shrimp from the sea,
Are good for our tummies - on that, we agree!

Do puffins swim and fly?

On leaving our nests, we fly out to sea.
Around 30 feet is how high we'll be.
Our wings act like fins, our feet act as rudders.
We swim really fast, to keep up with the others.

What are baby puffins called?

We're called little Pufflings when we first hatch.
Both parents care for us, sharing their catch.
Only one egg per couple is found in the nest.
With all that attention, we feel really blessed!

How many kinds of puffins are there?

Atlantic, Tufted, and Horned are our three main types.
There's even a cousin – "Rhinoceros,"   Oh, Yipes!

Are puffins endangered?

We have an awesome family, numbering 6 million or so.
That makes a lot of squawking kids – and that is what we know.
But our numbers are dropping; it's so sad to say.
It's harder to find our tiny food, day after day.
The oceans are warming because of pollution.
We hope you can help the world find a solution.

Where can I see puffins?

You can travel to Iceland to see me and my kin,
and you can also find books with pictures I'm in.

I'm glad we could share some news of our crew.
"So long for now; we PUFFINS LOVE YOU!"

SOURCES AND OTHER READINGS

Audubon Project. Puffins.
https://projectpuffin.audubon.org/birds/puffin-faqs

The Cornell Lab of Ornithology. Atlantic Puffins: life history.
https://www.allaboutbirds.org/guide/Atlantic_Puffin/lifehistory

Iceland on the Web. Puffins.
https://www.icelandontheweb.com/articles-on-iceland/nature/wildlife/puffins/

Atlantic Puffin - *Fratercula arctica*
https://nhpbs.org/natureworks/atlanticpuffin.htm

Vigur Island.
https://en.wikipedia.org/wiki/Vigur

ABOUT THE AUTHORS

Grandpa Bale, a native of Michigan, received an MD from the University of Michigan and held faculty positions at the Universities of Iowa and Utah. He enjoys fly fishing, photography, writing and travel. He and his wife Martha have five grandchildren.

Granddaddy Solms, a native of Georgia, attended Emory University, worked in employee relations and recently retired from the presidency of a business brokerage firm in North Carolina. He enjoys travel, photography and cooking. He and his wife Wendy have four granddaughters.